Weather

An Act of Man
Un-Natural Disasters

Michael Fleming

Since man ignited the first fire, there was smoke. Before the fire, there was no smoke. Before the pollution, there were no clouds. Before the man, there was no weather.

Man, however, is not the problem. Their arsonist-like obsessive use of combustion - is. There is an alternative, and there has been since the axis of the earth began to spin for them.

It's called: perpetual motion.

The Global Warming Hoax: The Cult of Fearmongering for Profit

Nearly half of the globe now disbelieves in man-made climate change. Of course man can affect the climate – but do they?

The answer is: yes. Intentionally, and unintentionally.

With pollution from factories, with intentional pollution from geoengineering and cloud seeding, with combustion engines – humans cause a drastic effect on the climate on a daily basis.

However, the geoengineering scheme of "combatting global warming" can be laid to rest.

Emissions of pollution, intentional destruction of the environment and the population, is researched by many former employees of Lawrence Livermore Lab. Those former employees, such as Ken Caldeira, researched ways to kill people – not save them.

Nuclear weapons testing of a sulfur-injected

atmosphere was performed in the 1950s and 1960s, and it has absolutely nothing to do with "global warming" this time – either.

Climatic Change (2008) 90:315–331
DOI 10.1007/s10584-008-9411-3

On geoengineering with sulphate aerosols in the tropical upper troposphere and lower stratosphere

A. F. Tuck · D. J. Donaldson · M. H. Hitchman ·
E. C. Richard · H. Tervahattu · V. Vaida · J. C. Wilson

Received: 21 February 2007 / Accepted: 19 February 2008 / Published online: 12 April 2008
© Springer Science + Business Media B.V. 2008

Abstract This paper is in response to the Editorial Essay by Crutzen and the Editorial Comment by Cicerone in the August 2006 issue of *Climatic Change*. We reprise the evidence from atmospheric nuclear weapon testing in the 1950s and 1960s which is salient to the mooted maintenance of an artificial sulphate aerosol layer in the lower stratosphere, including a hitherto and now posthumous unpublished analysis of the ^{185}W Hardtack data. We also review recent investigations by ourselves, which have considerable bearing on some relevant questions concerning meteorological dynamics, aerosol chemistry and physics and the photodissociation of stratospheric sulphuric acid.

1 Introduction

It has been proposed that in the event of a failure to reduce emission rates of carbon dioxide to the atmosphere from fossil fuel combustion, the radiative balance could be "geo-

The intentional modification of the environment, the intentional destruction of life on earth, will always see an equal and opposite reaction from physics.

No man would crap in his own bed – if he had the

sanity about himself to not desire to lie in his own feces. Such is geoengineering and cloud seeding.

The desire to harm another person requires a 72-hour mental evaluation. We have a 4% population who are "sociopathic," as mentioned, which is the most destructive form of mental illness that has ever existed. Unfortunately for them, and for most others, it is difficult to realize and understand someone that is a great liar without a conscious. For us 96%, we only see through the filter that someone else desires to help us – not harm us.

For cloud seeding and geoengineering, this is not the case.

As with the Climategate scandal, the leaked emails that stated "hide the decline" within Michael Mann's report, the modified hockey-stick chart, the recent drastic winters that we have been facing – it has become quite obvious to the perceptive.

The global warming fraud is laid to rest. However, the pollution conundrum continues.

If pollution were ceased, the globe would warm for a short period. This, however, would not cause "natural disasters" as cloud-seeding employees so luxuriously blame their murder on.

The globe could warm 5 degrees, and we would see nothing more than a new Victorian age.

The "drought" scheme is the best excuse that I have heard for cloud seeding thus far. However, since the dawn of man, Earth has watered its own plants naturally with mist and fog.

What makes man think that they can do a better job by controlling something that has been around for a lot longer than they have? They know better. It is simply the feeling of power that drives people to control. Nothing more, nothing less.

Clouds Are Man-Made

"Fair Weather Clouds Hold Dirty Secret"

http://asr.science.energy.gov/science/research-highlights/RNDc5/view

Geoengineering and Cloud Seeding

Monika, an elderly lady from Münchenerin, plunges to her death from a hot-air balloon. Before her last breath draws from her frail body, her pain serves as a reminder to what is important in life.

Her agony, her senseless and meaningless torture, was not "in vain." She spent 53 years on earth as a happy girl, then lady, then elderly inspiration. She wanted to live her life out, as the other elderly in Germany, serving as an example to the youth – and a grandmother to the grandmother-less.

In 2008, Monika began to suffer. Her bed-sheets were covered in fibers, her friends called her "delusional," both her doctor and the Federal Bureau of Investigation claimed "no knowledge" of the source of her disease. She is not alone.

Over 14,000 people are diagnosed with Morgellons disease in America, and it is estimated that millions more have the disease – and assumed that the entire global population has been affected by it. Monika will no longer see her family. Monika will no longer enjoy her life. Monika ended her life – as she could no longer enjoy it – thanks to some who destroyed it.

Stories such as this one are far too common and should not happen. People have the power to change what is seen, and people should also have the courage to stand against it. No person should end up like Monika, and no person should suffer as she did. This problem can be solved, though like Monika's case, it will be neither quick nor easy.

The purpose of this proposal to end geoengineering and cloud seeding is to convince the readers that truth is stranger than fiction. Their assumptions of a "cloudy" forecast are as their delusions of an "act of God" creating tornadoes.

The problem of permissible pollution and the outcome of various "cloud seeding" experiments has murdered countless individuals for over a century. The admissions of TWMA (2010), NOAA (2006), and NASA (1996), who are all participants in this cloud seeding and geoengineering scheme, will establish my credibility; although it is merely a criminal admitting to a crime.

Everyone is affected by the weather. It it often said, "people talk about the weather, but never do anything about it." Most people believe that when they look up, they see a cloud. Most people believe that when they look up, they see a contrail. Neither is true, and neither of those forms of "nature" exist.

Cloud seeding and geoengineering should be abolished, investigated, and prosecuted – as these programs have murdered countless numbers of people, have led to the destruction of billions of dollars in land, homes, and businesses – and are a liability to national security and existence as human beings.

This problem began in the 1800s. Though many people may argue that "there was cloudy weather before the 1800s," America is, unfortunately, becoming more and more like the genocidal mongrels in Communist China. Also, no cloud that we will ever lay eyes upon – is "natural," but rather man-made.

The first cloud seeding experiments (in Texas), took

place in 1891. After noticing that the Civil War bombardments and shellings produced rain, Texas generals decided to "break the balanced state of nature" by reproducing the effect of gunpowder shellings into the sky. In 1923, aircraft began to enhance these cloud-seeding projects with silver iodide, cooperating with the ground-seeding technique, with the ability to target specific cities and locations with rainfall.

The question is: why? This is very simple to answer. Four percent of Americans are diagnosed as a "sociopath." Over twelve-million Americans are labeled as having "no conscious," and no regard for human life.

Cloud seeding and geoengineering is nothing more than a control-freak, similar to a wife-beater, who seeks power over the feeble and weak, while playing God with Mother Earth. There is simply no other excuse for weather modification, as there never has been – and never will be.

So, people are left with the question "are any clouds

formed naturally?" Some say that "schools teach that clouds form from condensation, and the sunlight causes clouds to form by evaporation." Science begs to differ. According to physics, Homogenus (water-only clouds) can only be produced in a laboratory, and do not form naturally in the atmosphere. In addition, clouds require Cloud Condensation Nuclei to form, which consists of soot, sulfur, or salt. The only "natural" cloud that will ever be produced by Earth, is from a volcanic eruption or fire. Fog is natural, fog is condensation. Clouds, however, are atmospheric balls of pollution. When cloud condensation nuclei are released into the atmosphere, water attaches to them from humidity and forced cloud-seeding, and will produce rainfall (eventually). This is how forest fires are able to "put themselves out."

Another problem generated by cloud seeding is that deaths, by the millions, occur every single year. We will never know the true death toll from cloud-seeding, but as the World Health Organization stated in 2012, 7 million people (1 out of 8) died from pollution-related ailments alone. This does not include accidents attributed to weather, injuries, tornadoes, hurricanes, and any other "natural disaster" that is blamed on "an act of God."

However, most cults, including the climate cult, do blame their actions on God. If clouds formed naturally, if the assumption that "water evaporates to the atmosphere to form a cloud" were true, it would be accepted as "natural disasters" or an "act of God." However, this is far from the truth. Cloud condensation nuclei consist of sulfur dioxide, soot, and similar pollution.

Without cloud condensation nuclei, clouds cannot form. Cloud condensation nuclei as mentioned, are seeds for cloud growth. When forests are burned, it rains. There is absolutely no difference between the destruction of the earth and the destruction of another human being – as they all are correlated factors – considering that we must live together on Earth – and without our life-sustaining planet – we cannot survive.

To make a claim that states "Earth's clouds are not

real" should warrant sufficient evidence, correct? The reality is, only a few hundred years ago, a blue sky was what everyone on this planet was able to enjoy. Two laws of physics, which agree with my statement: the Kelvin effect and Raoult's Law, state that "supersaturation required in the atmosphere to produce a cloud, naturally, is approximately 400%."

In the natural coolness of the atmosphere, the wind and gravity effects of natural fog on earth, the Earth's atmosphere remains below 2% supersaturation. Without atmospheric forcing or a volcanic eruption, no cloud will ever form over a blue sky. Since man built the first fire, man burned the first forest, man caused his own destruction with cloud seeding. What was once a beautiful, blue sky – is now a haze over humanity.

One effect of cloud seeding which one should particularly detest, is the obvious potential for death.

Who can look at someone die, even on television, without compassion? Better yet, who can kill someone –

and do it again the next day? Anyone who actively and knowingly seeds clouds, whether as part of a government organization or as an indirect pollutant of society (i.e. power plants), knowingly participates in murder.

Obviously, anyone who repeats murder is a serial killer. There are less cloud seeding bases in America than there are deaths from cloud seeding on a daily basis. Thus, each cloud seeding base is responsible for at least one death that day, on average, and continues to seed clouds again – the very next day.

One excuse for cloud seeding is "drought." Another excuse is "a military operation." Another excuse is "global warming." All of these excuses for cloud seeding and geoengineering, simply by reminding people of how it all began. Fog dispersal was used to clear the air for visibility of military aircraft. Rain was produced in Operation Popeye, during Vietnam, to rain on peaceful protesters who planned to disrupt the war with love and peace signs. Not to mention, most deaths were caused by infection in

Vietnam, from Bioprecipitation, which is gram-negative soil bacteria or "dust" used to produce rain. In addition, the Bay of Pigs invasion failed due to cloud seeding, causing the deaths of hundreds of people.

As for "global warming," we are actually facing a global cooling. I will remind us of the "Climategate" scandal, which proves that our temperature has actually declined in recent years, and we are suffering from no potential threat of a "carbon dioxide attributed rise in temperature."

Regardless of excuses, there is no excuse for rape. The Earth did not ask for pollution in its blue eye, and we did not ask for pollution in our blue sky.

Another effect is the toxicity of the soil, migration of the bees to their own death (and thus, ours), and the destruction of soil and the toxicity of our crops and food supply. The toxicity of the soil from sulfur dioxide, aluminum particulates, strontium, and fungus – yes, fungus is used in cloud seeding – is rather disturbing and destructive. Bioprecipitation, as mentioned, is the process of using "rain-making bacteria" to produce a dusty atmosphere, which will collect any available condensation in conjunction with cloud condensation nuclei, and produce rainfall. While some claim that "acid rain" is a rare occurrence, the very cause of acid rain is sulfur dioxide; and that sulfur dioxide is the main source of cloud condensation nuclei. Not to mention, the very cause of "global warming," the non-existent rise in temperature, is Carbon Dioxide. According to every single cloud seeding organization that does not use aircraft-based sources, dry-ice (frozen Carbon Dioxide), is the main (ground-based) cloud-seeding ingredient. While our nation fakes the reduction of Carbon emissions, taxing Americans for breathing out with "Carbon Credits," federally-funded cloud seeding operations are performed with a $1.5 million federal budget, which does not include state budgets; hence, state-funding accounting for most of the cloud seeding monetary input. This fact also clarifies the excuse of a "military operation." No soldier will be deployed to attack their own citizens. This is why military intelligence operatives, who have a history of treason, will be deployed to further research into geoengineering.

As we saw with the tornado in Joplin Missouri, as we saw with Hurricane Sandy, as we watch the Philippines Typhoon on television; real people are displaced. Real people die. People are accustomed to viewing these people through a television set, through a news story.

These are real people, with real lives, real families, and real memories – and are no more important than others. For someone to allow another person to die is to allow our their death. For someone to allow millions of people to be displaced in one day, from one cloud-seeded storm, and yet to understand the mentality of those who perform this disgusting program – would be beyond foolish.

What did our justice system do to Charles Manson? Timothy McVeigh? We placed them in prison, as the serial killer sociopaths that they are. We had to do such to prevent future crimes performed by such mindless and cruel individuals. As with an animal that cannot be controlled in society, if a bear is loose in a neighborhood – we must call animal control to put it in its place so that no residents are harmed.

Now that this very simple fact that "no clouds are natural" has been presented, who will rise against the serial killers? Who will believe that it is for a "drought," for "global warming," who will be the next to ride in the serial killer's car to the edge of the woods? Are people foolish enough to hitchhike with Ted Bundy… again?

Will Monika's death be "in vain?" Why did she question this in her suicide note? Was she attention-seeking for herself with an act of suicide, or as a cry for desperate help in unspeakable pain and torment? Who does her death benefit? Herself? Every crime has a motive. Why would someone dump fungus on the world? Sounds crazy – doesn't it? We live in a world with 4%

people diagnosed as a sociopath with no conscious, who think that it is "funny" to harm and destroy the other 96%. We live in a world where power is measured by a comma in the bank account, where happiness is measured in numbers. How could destroying the planet create profit? How could releasing a Monsanto transformation-method-patented fiber, agrobacterium tumefaciens (rhizobium radiobacter) / Morgellons, profit organizations and individuals who perform these cruel acts? This is the reality of monopolies, this is how business works – this is how some people are. As unfortunate as it is, we can only expose the truth in hopes that it will change. 1891 was the first year of government-funded cloud seeding, and the beginning of a destructive era for America.

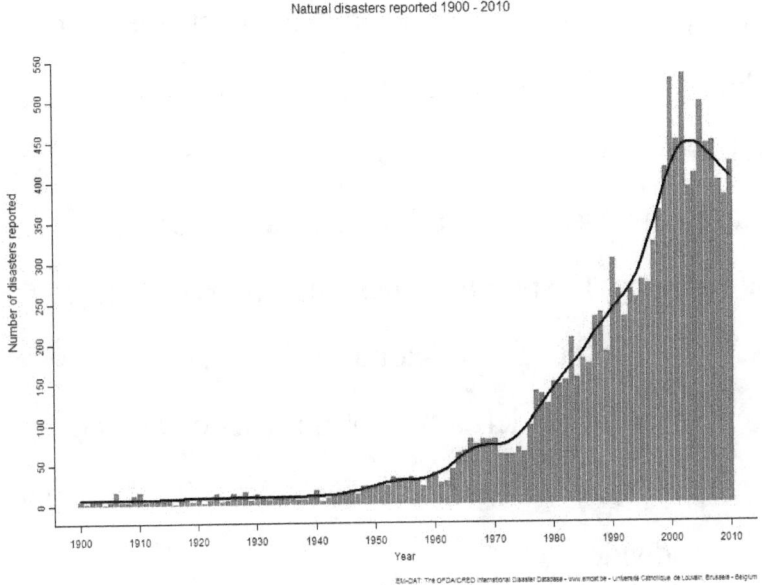

Figure 1: Natural Disasters Reported 1900-2009, (EM-DAT) 2009.

Figure 1: Coorelation of "natural disasters" since the conception of cloud seeding. Source: EM-DAT: Natural Disasters (2009).

As shown in Figure 1, cloud seeding experiments began in 1891, and the above image reflects the account of "natural disasters" including floods, tornadoes, hurricanes, and other events as the cloud seeding program began to increase and multiply to other states and organizations. Despite their best intentions of "playing God" with Mother Earth, cloud seeding and geoengineering has left a trail of destruction and death along the way, killing approximately 20,000 people per day, worldwide.

The best plan to solve the cloud seeding and geoengineering problem is educating the public about the reality of manufactured weather, plan for alternative and reliable sources of water, and use sustainability of renewable resources (which are plentiful); rather than relying on a temporary solution for a permanent problem.

Because cloud seeding and geoengineering have caused (and continue to cause) massive deaths, and do so on a daily basis, people should treat any cloud seeding project as an emergency-attention need. When someone is being murdered, we dial 911. When 40% of the population is dying from air quality, people need absolute emergency intervention to these obviously destructive and deadly forces that threaten our very existence. The public should also find reliable alternatives to water sources for man-made farms who wish to mass-produce food, such as government grants for farming irrigation techniques. When cloud seeding is used to produce rain, rather than irrigation, the farmer is not the only one who receives the acidic water on his land; as roads, homes, and schools are drowned in acid rain. Thus, when cloud seeding "waters the plains," so to speak, it is nothing more than "playing God" with an Ant Farm – but some kids who liked to "shake it up" never "grew up." Ending cloud seeding would ironically, as shown in the next section, end drought as well as stabilize the climate to a natural state of the earth's cycle – in conjunction with the orbit of the sun (Hołyst, 2013). The main benefit of ending cloud seeding and geoengineering is to allow the continuing sustainability of life that our planet has produced for the population for generations.

These solutions are better than proposed cloud seeding and geoengineering schemes, since these remedies would not only cost much less – but would also create jobs and increase the health of our planet and its inhabitants. The health benefits of humans are highly affected by cloud seeding and geoengineering, as 1 out of every 8 humans die from air pollution; while 40% of deaths are attributed to air-pollution related causes (Pokharel, 2010). While carbon dioxide is emitted in the form of "poof" clouds, sulfur dioxide is emitted to "counteract it" with further pollution. Both programs equally contribute to the death of humans in this case. In addition, weather modification programs have displaced millions, destroyed many third-world nations, and have cost insurance companies billions – which eventually leads to the collapse of a corporation, one-by-one, and then an economy in its entirety. Of course, ending cloud seeding and geoengineering would be a rather difficult task to accomplish – as nearly ⅔ of nations participate in this scheme; with the most active being Communist nations, such as Russia and China. By simply engaging the public with the truth about their weather, about the man-made clouds that form man-made storms, a decision can be made based upon simple facts. When people assume that their weather was formed from water, as it may have been "natural" as taught, it completely distracts from the logic of cloud seeding and geoengineering – which, without volcanic activity or fire, are required to produce any type of clouds that are now seen on earth.

There are three steps to making this idea a reality. First, there must be alternative energy sources. Combustion-energy production must cease immediately, as there are many, many sources of perpetual-motion production capabilities that can provide a higher over-unity production as well as a non-pollutant source of production.

Next, cloud seeding bases and geoengineering sources must be closed and investigated for potential further use. With any cloud seeding scheme, unfortunately, the person who is creating the storm is intentionally and knowingly committing a crime of destruction. People cannot ignore reality and pretend that this is an "act of God" when science refutes the obvious. We cannot deny logic, we must face reality head-on, and understand that any weather modification activity is murder. Finally, we must educate the public about the reality of the atmosphere.

For over a century, we have been made to believe that any weather is natural – which is only false in the case of the four seasons with the earth's rotation. If we truly understood the death toll from cloud seeding – the cancer caused by humidity and sulfates, the infections from bioprecipitation, the overall affect of pollution and carbon nanotubes on the human population and their life spans in general – the people would take immediate action against it. Humanity cannot live in denial to change the future; and if it repeats the past, it will continue to see the same results.

This plan will help to save human lives and the future generations of those who wish to live. Additionally, this plan will put to better use the collective sustainability of humanity who are caught up in the "band-aid on a scar" phase (Pokharel, 2014). Humanity must put the past behind us, and recreate the present – so that we are able to live in the future. The most costly storm that has been produced by cloud seeding in recent years was Hurricane Sandy. The monetary destruction caused by this engineered storm, alone, could have provided every farmer with irrigation tools for lifetime – as well as tools to plow their land, house their crops, and generate decades of food for the entire nation. As seen in the chart, death tolls from weather modification have drastically reduced in recent years; indicating that humanity is beginning to wake up to the reality of the murder and destruction caused by manufactured storms. However, the genocide of pollution remains. A system that was given to us, a life-sustaining planet with clear blue skies, the smell of flowers in the morning, the morning fog that waters the earth naturally – and the ability to enjoy such without the threat of sulfur dioxide emissions – is where we need to be.

The daily calculation of deaths per day that can be directly attributed to cloud seeding and other pollution methods, such as combustion energy (transportation, coal burning, etcetera included) is 19,880.

Let's help our society to reclaim our clean air and our blue sky. It will help to stop the innocent death of asthmatics, reduce health costs and doctors' visits, and not force them to worry about the future with self-sustaining and pollution-free methods of energy production. We were given a rich land to support life, yet – if we destroy it – we must also remember that we "make the bed today that we will lie in tonight."

Cloud seeding and geoengineering have caused enough deaths, diseases, and famines. It's time that we close the chapter on control, and open the chapter on oneness. To regain our skies, we must realize – every day should be a "sunny" day.

The Pollution Holocaust:
Chemical Terrorism with Sulfur Dioxide

As far back as Napoleon, sulfur dioxide has been used for genocide. In fact, Napoleon gassed many slaves within the hulls of ships with sulfur dioxide – leading to the slaughter of over 100,000 Caribbean slaves (Haitians).

See:

http://www.telegraph.co.uk/news/worldnews/europe/franc e/1504014/Napoleons-genocide-on-a-par-with-Hitler.html

With as many as 40% of people dying from air pollution, this should be a cause of concern for every single human. No matter who you are – everyone will be affected by air pollution – sometime within their lifetime. When 2 out of 5 people presently die from air pollution, the reality is – at least one of every person's family members will succumb to the negative effects of pollution.

See:

*http://www.sciencedaily.com/releases/2007/08/07081316
2438.htm*

In America, we have enough funds, enough technology, and enough resources to end every single particulate of pollution in our nation. We even have an organization designed to ensure that this happens, called the "Environmental Protection Agency." Why do over 200,000 Americans die from air pollution yearly? Worldwide, the number is well over 7 million.

See: http://lae.mit.edu/air-pollution-causes-200000-early-deaths-each-year-in-the-u-s/

Automobiles, planes, trains, and other combustion engines produce a large portion of pollution. Energy production with combustion methods produce even more. However, the number one cause of pollution is: you guessed it – geoengineering.

See: http://sth.sagepub.com/content/36/2/190.short

The intentional addition of atmospheric pollutants to

the air, especially with sulfur dioxide, is obviously an act of murder. Quite actually, on a daily basis, we can call it "genocide." Serial killing would be a light term to use for each drone operator who performs such disgusting acts of cruelty.

So, we have Napoleon, Hitler – who's next? With 7 million dead in 2012 from pollution alone… we all know the reality by now. There is no "disinformation campaign" that can serve as an insanity plea for the geoengineers. There is no "global warming" excuse that they can now use to keep gassing the population with sulfur dioxide.

The reality is… we all know better. It's time to do more than we know. Act, rather than observe. This should have been ended before it started – but unfortunately, we are allowing history to repeat itself.

We can only hope for the sake of humanity, that we are able to look back on this, one day – just as Hitler's holocaust, and say to ourselves "I'm glad that's over. You see how those people were? What freaks. I'm glad we've evolved since then."

When Dorothy in the Wizard of Oz struggled to find the person who created her tornado and destroyed her home finally found the "man behind the curtain," it was rather easy to see that he was nothing more than a deranged and delusional psychopath – who simply wanted to appear powerful by using various techniques to make himself look like a "big man."

"Pay no attention to the man behind the curtain," he said with a gruff voice.

When people are asked about geoengineering, there never seems to be an accurate finger-point. Why is that?

What I always seem to hear is the word "they."

"They are spraying us with chemtrails."

Who are "they?"

Let's explore.

"Several notable organizations have investigated geoengineering with a view to evaluating its potential, including the US Congress, NASA, the Royal Society, the Institute of Mechanical Engineers,and the UK Parliament. The Asilomar International Conference on Climate Intervention Technologies was convened to identify and develop risk reduction guidelines for climate intervention experimentation. Several geoengineering strategies have been proposed. IPCC documents detail several notable proposals.These fall into two main categories: solar radiation management and carbon dioxide removal. However, other proposals exist. The Geoengineering Climate: Technical Evaluation and Discussion of Impacts project of the National Academy of Sciences funded by United States agencies, including NOAA, NASA, and the CIA, commenced in March 2013, is expected to issue a report in fall 2014. "An ad hoc committee will conduct a technical evaluation of a limited number *of proposed geoengineering techniques, including examples of both solar radiation management (SRM) and carbon dioxide removal (CDR) techniques, and comment generally on the potential impacts of deploying these technologies, including possible environmental, economic, and national security concerns. The study will:*

Evaluate what is currently known about the science of several (3-4) selected example techniques, including potential risks and consequences (both intended and unintended), such as impacts, or lack thereof, on ocean acidification, describe what is known about the viability for implementation of the proposed techniques including technological and cost considerations, briefly explain other geoengineering technologies that have been proposed (beyond the selected examples), and identify future research needed to provide a credible scientific underpinning for future discussions.

The study will also discuss historical examples of related technologies (e.g., cloud seeding and other weather modification) for lessons that might be learned about societal reactions, examine what international agreements exist which may be relevant to the experimental testing or deployment of geoengineering technologies, and briefly explore potential societal and ethical considerations related to geoengineering. This study is intended to provide a careful, clear scientific foundation that informs ethical, legal, and political discussions surrounding geoengineering. The project has support from the National Academy of Sciences, the U.S. intelligence community, the National Oceanic and Atmospheric Administration, and the National Aeronautics and Space Administration. The approximate start date for the project is March 2013; a report is expected be issued in fall 2014."

- Wikipedia, Climate Engineering
http://en.wikipedia.org/wiki/Climate_engineering

There are many organizations investigating the use of chemical terrorism and weather warfare. This is a global program – a global scheme. There is no one organization to point the finger at. However, NASA has been appointed to "head" the geoengineering program.

For more information on the blatant discussion of chemical terrorism use against citizens, see Google Groups "GEO." Headed by Andrew Lockley, a "financial advisor" who knows just as much about the climate as a troll at the end of a rainbow.

See:

http://news.sciencemag.org/2009/03/darpa-explore-geoengineering

http://www.popsci.com/technology/article/2013-07/spooks-look-mad-science-global-warming-solution

Dispelling the "Contrail" Myth

Aside from the fact that geoengineering is a current program in testing phase, we still have a few non-believers in chemical terrorism, who simply label the trails in the sky as "contrails," or "condensation trails."

Unfortunately, those folks must take a step towards reality before we are able to face it head on. There is no such thing as a "condensation trail" of water that emits from a jet engine. If water is coming from any combustion engine, of any kind, whether vehicle or aircraft, the engine would not be in operation.

Why? Because combustion engines rely on combustion, which is burning – and water does just the opposite.

In fact, within most planes, kerosene is used as jet fuel. If water is added to this fuel, the combustion engine will not operate. Now that we have dispelled the "contrail" myth, let us dig deeper into what aircraft emissions actually consist of:

"An exhaust system is usually piping used to guide reaction exhaust gases away from a controlled combustion inside an engine ... [and] must be carefully designed to carry toxic and/or noxious gases away from the users of the machine." - Wikipedia, Exhaust System

We have two types of geoengineering:

1) Intentional geoengineering with installed manifests.

2) Unintentional or "contracted" geoengineering, fuel additives that contain chemicals

"JP-8 is formulated with icing inhibitor, corrosion inhibitors, lubricants, and antistatic agents, and less benzene (a carcinogen) and less n-hexane (a neurotoxin) than JP-4. However, it also smells stronger than JP-4. JP-

8 has an oily feel to the touch, while JP-4 feels more like a solvent." -Wikipedia, JP-8

So, we have officially dispelled the "contrail" myth with a simple scientific understanding of an exhaust system. It is a well-known fact that condensation trails can only form at an altitude above 50,000 feet. However, using this simple analogy of "water from combustion engines is ignorant" might help us ward off a few trolls in the future.

One other argument that a person might portray, is that air consists of oxygen – and fuel within aircraft contain hydrogen. When combining hydrogen emissions plus oxygen, you may see a condensation trail form from the aircraft.

However, the amount of oxygen at 50,000 feet is not enough to produce a condensation trail. In addition, Hydrogen is no longer used in aircraft fuel.

At 50000ft, the standard barometric pressure is13 kPa (99 mmHg). This means that there is 13% of the oxygen available at sea level.

http://www.altitude.org/air_pressure.php

The simple fact is, according to science, any trail left behind any aircraft – is a chemical. Regardless of length, persistence, or excuse – it is a chemical – and the FAA should be contacted immediately to report a "smoking aircraft."

Geoengineering is illegal. The "global warming" scheme has failed. We all know better, by now. It would take a truly insane and delusional human being, an extremely sociopathic and demented individual, a "mad scientist" or "serial killer," if you will, to ever promote "spraying pollution to combat 'global warming.'"

Now, again, we all know better. Time to do something about it.

For a list of official tests that have been performed within recent years, see Wikipedia "Climate Engineering."

Multiple firms, including the Central Intelligence

Agency and NASA, have participated in chemical terrorism tests on the public population. For more information into previous tests, see "chaff (countermeasure)."

Regardless of what chemical is in the sky, geoengineering is an intentional addition of chemicals to the atmosphere, to the public's air supply, and to our breathing space. As in the 1950 Supreme Court Case "*Southwest Weather Research, Inc. v. Duncan,*" no cloud seeding activities are allowed to take place over the unconsenting population. Doing so is a trespass, and cloud seeding is, according to federal law, a "nuisance" in 48 out of 50 states.

See: http://scholarship.law.duke.edu/dlj/vol9/iss2/11/ (Download PDF)

The problem that we are now facing is "global dimming," and extreme health issues from the exhaust produced by aircraft, which use chemicals other than simple jet fuel, and especially from geoengineering and cloud seeding – the intentional and deliberate addition of chemicals to our air supply.

See:

http://www.bbc.co.uk/sn/tvradio/programmes/horizon/dim ming_trans.shtml

These "tests" are nothing new. In fact, the first successful aircraft cloud seeding experiment was performed in 1923. Ground cloud seeding experiments have taken place since last century. For anyone to deny this, or simply state that what you are seeing is "condensation," is nothing more than the denial phase of their own demise.

Atmosphere Modification: HAARP

(High Frequency Active Auroral Research Program)

	Amplitude modulation	Beam painting	Geometric modulation
Symmetric	Vertical-AM	Grid-paint	Circle-sweep
Directed	Oblique-AM	Line-paint	Sawtooth-sweep

What is it like to "play God?" What would it be like to murder someone – or destroy an entire town – from a safe distance, while never answering for what you have to do? Just ask the guys at HAARP.

The above photo shows what HAARP is able to do

with an ionospheric heater. Note the word "heater." Electromagnetic fields are directed at a portion of the atmosphere, which when reflected, are able to target specific areas with weather patterns. This is an obvious weather-control research pattern – and has proven to be extremely destructive over recent years.

Dunes in the Empty Quarter, 1,000 mile area of dunes and desert, not crossed until 20th century, Arabian Peninsula, Sultanate of

The "coincidences" attributed to the use of HAARP, combined with the time anomalies of their atmospheric heater activation, are – according to probability and statistics – related to HAARP itself. HAARP has recently removed their magnetometer (the measure of EMF ejection) from the public view, and is no longer available on their website.

The massive earthquake of Japan, and the Tsunami of Haiti are events directly attributed to HAARP – just to name a few. With the last few years of extreme weather patterns, we are left with no "coincidences" when it comes to this machine of destruction.

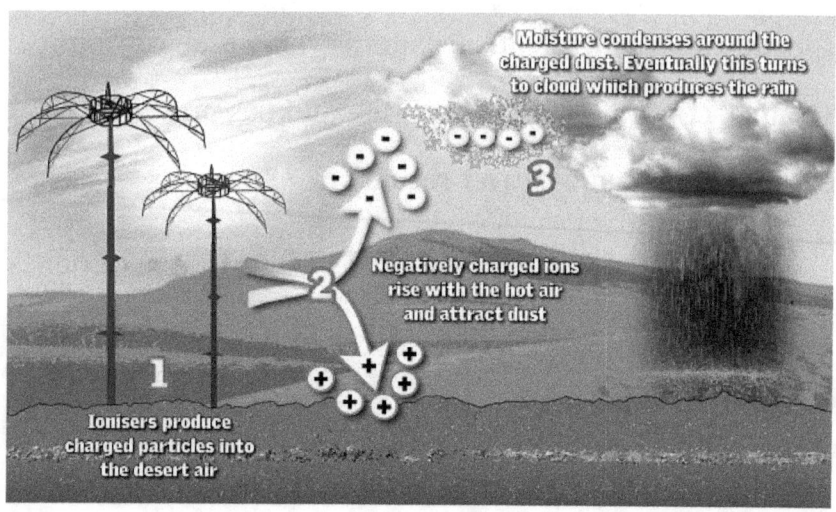

In addition, the High Frequency Active Auroral Research Program uses the protection of a military name to perform their acts of weather warfare (http://fas.org/spp/military/docops/usaf/2025/v3c15/v3c15-1.htm). However, these are not "soldiers." These are a group of experimental "scientists" with no more knowledge of the atmosphere than many high-school students (http://vlf.stanford.edu/research/experiments-haarp-ionospheric-heater).

We are left to reap the "benefits" of this project, and left paying the check for our own (intentional) destruction.

Obviously, cloud seeding and geoengineering are the two basic causes of every storm. Because, according to physics, clouds cannot form naturally on earth (http://en.wikipedia.org/wiki/Cloud_physics). However, these "tests" within the atmosphere are able to control and steer weather patterns, and this is the exact stated purpose of this facility (http://www.businessweek.com/stories/2005-10-19/who-controls-the-weather).

Regardless of cloud seeding, geoengineering, or directed ionospheric-heater testing – all weather modification is banned, globally. See our "Weather Modification History" page for more details.

Unfortunately, with the removal of the magnetometer from public view, it is no longer to prove that HAARP created any weather pattern within a particular area. HAARP had a North, South, East, and West grid for each of their locations in Alaska. When the magnetometer was online – it was a rather simple process.

Now, we are only left to speculate. One thing is for sure – HAARP should be closed. There is absolutely no purpose for this waste of Federal tax dollars, and it is in blatant violation of American laws and of International Weather Modification treaties.

"Facts are facts, independent of any consciousness. No amount of passionate wishing, desperate longing or hopeful pleading can alter the facts. Nor will ignoring or evading the facts erase them: the facts remain, immutable."

-Ayn Rand

References

Geoengineering sparks international ban, first-ever congressional report

http://www.washingtonpost.com/wp-dyn/content/article/2010/10/29/AR2010102906365.html

Climate Intelligence Agency: The CIA is now funding research into manipulating the climate.

http://www.slate.com/articles/technology/future_tense/2013/07/cia_funds_nas_study_into_geoengineering_and_climate_change.html

http://www.sciencedaily.com/releases/2007/08/070813162438.htm

Climatic Change (Impact Factor: 3.63). 01/2008; 90(3):315-331. DOI: 10.1007/s10584-008-9411-3

ABSTRACT This paper is in response to the Editorial Essay by Crutzen and the Editorial Comment by Cicerone in the August 2006 issue of Climatic Change. We reprise the evidence from atmospheric nuclear weapon testing in the 1950s and 1960s which is salient to the mooted maintenance of an artificial sulphate aerosol layer in the lower stratosphere, including a hitherto and now posthumous unpublished analysis of the 185W Hardtack data. We also review recent investigations by ourselves, which have considerable bearing on some relevant questions concerning meteorological dynamics, aerosol chemistry and physics and the photodissociation of stratospheric sulphuric acid.

http://www.researchgate.net/publication/225824392_On_geoengineering_with_sulphate_aerosols_in_the_tropical_upper_troposph ere_and_lower_stratosphere

http://www.tshaonline.org/handbook/online/articles/ymwed

http://en.wikipedia.org/wiki/Cloud_physics

http://en.wikipedia.org/wiki/Climate_engineering

http://en.wikipedia.org/wiki/Stratospheric_sulfur_aerosols_(geoen gineering)

http://en.wikipedia.org/wiki/Weather_modification

http://en.wikipedia.org/wiki/Geoengineering

http://en.wikipedia.org/wiki/Stratospheric_Particle_Injection_for_Climate_Engineering

http://en.wikipedia.org/wiki/Solar_radiation_management

http://en.wikipedia.org/wiki/Charged_Aerosol_Release_Experime nt

http://en.wikipedia.org/wiki/Nuclear_weapons_testing

Binod Pokharel, Bart Geerts, Xiaoqin Jing, Katja Friedrich, Joshua Aikins, Daniel Breed, Roy Rasmussen, Arlen Huggins. (2014) The impact of ground-based glaciogenic seeding on clouds and precipitation over mountains: A multi-sensor case study of shallow precipitating orographic cumuli. Atmospheric Research 147-148, 162-182.

R Hołyst, M Litniewski, D Jakubczyk, K Kolwas, M Kolwas, K Kowalski, S Migacz, S Palesa, M Zientara. (2013) Evaporation of freely suspended single droplets: experimental, theoretical and computational simulations. Reports on Progress in Physics 76:3, 034601.

University of Rochester Medical Center. (2014, June 5). New evidence links air pollution to autism, schizophrenia. ScienceDaily. Retrieved June 10, 2014 from www.sciencedaily.com/releases/2014/06/140605155722.htm

American Heart Association. (2010, May 11). Evidence growing of air pollution's link to heart disease, death. ScienceDaily. Retrieved June 10, 2014 from www.sciencedaily.com/releases/2010/05/100510161244.htm

Eugene M. Emme, comp., Aeronautics and Astronautics: An American Chronology of Science and Technology in the Exploration of Space, 1915-1960 (Washington, DC: National Aeronautics and Space Administration, 1961), pp. 11-19.

http://www.ess.uci.edu/~cpasquer/classes/ess200b/pdfs/cloud_microphysics.pdf

http://www.bt.com.bn/science-technology/2010/05/26/un-urges-caution-synthetic-life-forms

http://www.rtcc.org/2012/10/18/un-agreement-urges-caution-over-geoengineering-tests/

http://www.tz.de/muenchen/stadt/egling-verzweiflungstat-wegen-raetselhafter-krankheit-mein-soll-nicht-umsonst-sein-tz-878295.html

http://clouds.wikia.com/wiki/Cirrus_aviaticus

http://www.tshaonline.org/handbook/online/articles/ymwed

http://www.washingtonsblog.com/2012/08/as-many-as-12-million-americans-are-sociopaths.html

http://www.srh.noaa.gov/jetstream/clouds/formation.htm

http://humantouchofchemistry.com/all-you-ever-wanted-to-know-about-cloud-seeding.htm

http://www.pnl.gov/science/highlights/highlight.asp?id=1375

http://www.iop.org/resources/topic/archive/cloud/index.html

http://www.ucar.edu/communications/gcip/m8clclchange/m8pdfc1.pdf

http://www.realclearscience.com/2011/05/25/bioprecipitation_do_bacteria_create_hail_stones_241309.html

http://www.britannica.com/blogs/2009/01/4-kennedys-failure-at-the-bay-of-pigs-top-10-mistakes-by-us-presidents/

http://www.weathermodification.org/faq.php

http://www.bbc.com/future/story/20130304-the-trouble-with-cloud-seeding

http://qz.com/138141/china-creates-55-billion-tons-of-artificial-rain-a-year-and-it-plans-to-quintuple-that/

About the author

Michael D. Fleming (1983-[hasn't croaked yet]) was born in Bristol, Tennessee, to Native-American (Cherokee) and German descent, and grew up in Johnson City, Tennessee.

Michael's short-books cover various subjects, including government corruption, perpetual motion, and natural health remedies. All in all, Michael writes about the changes that he wishes for the betterment of society – and a promise of a new tomorrow.

Self-published and independent works.

Check out other titles at:
www.MichaelDavidFleming.com

This information is also available online at:
www.stopchemicalterrorism.com